R

is for

Relationship

Magick

Kitchen Table Magick Series

by
G. Alan Joel

Esoteric School of Shamanism & Magic

Email: *alan@shamanschool.com*
Website: *www.shamanschool.com*

Publisher: Esoteric School of Shamanism and Magic, Inc.

Disclaimer and Legal Notice:
The Esoteric School of Shamanism and Magic has made every effort to ensure, at the time of this writing, that the information contained in this book is as accurate as possible. The publisher and author make no warranties or representation with respect to the completeness, fitness, accuracy, applicability, or appropriateness of this book's contents. This book's information is provided strictly for entertainment and educational purposes. Should you choose to use or apply the ideas provided in this book, you take full responsibility for your own actions. The publisher and author provide no guarantee that your life will improve in any way should you choose to use the information presented in this book. The ability of the information provided in this book to provide self-help and life improvement to the reader is entirely dependent upon the reader. The reader's ability to gain positive results from the information presented in this book is entirely dependent on the amount of time the reader devotes to the application of the material in this book, the willingness of the reader to dedicate time and effort to learning the materials presented in this book, as well as the reader's own belief system, which may help or hinder the reader's ability to benefit from this book's materials. Since each reader differs according to willingness and openness to the information available in this book, the author and publisher cannot guarantee success or improvement for every individual reader. Neither the publisher nor the author assumes responsibility for the reader's actions, or whether the information is used for negative or positive purposes. The information contained in this book is drawn from tribal traditions—both modern and ancient—as well as the author's 30 plus years' experience researching and teaching this material to students. The information in this book is presented as interpreted by the author, and, as such, may or may not be entirely accurate. In no way should the information presented in this book be a substitute for advice from health or mental health professionals. The author and publisher are not liable—or in any way responsible—for actions

that the reader may or may not take as a result of reading the information contained in this book. The reader assumes full responsibility for his or her own actions and choices with regard to how he or she chooses to use the information in this book. The reader is strongly encouraged to choose to use the information provided in this book responsibly.

[this page intentionally left blank]

Relationship Magick Blessing

Child of Wonder,
Child of Flame
Nourish Our Spirits and
Protect Our Aim.

Having harmony in relationships be not the easiest to
achieve.
In fact, many would say that relationships woes be difficult
to relieve.
But worry not, magick is here to rescue the way you relate,
From perpetual everyday problems, from children and
money to dates!

Relationship magick helps you develop your inner senses,
So when life is in turmoil, you find solutions for harmony
rather than defenses.
From flower power to conscious choice exercises,
Relationship magick can help you be your wisest.

Having a difficult time communicating with children or your
boss?
Let the Chalice and Wand reach them through Spirit, without
fight or loss.

The Nighttime Blessing ritual brings harmony to the whole tribe,
While Question Circles provide needed answers with just the right vibe!

Thus, my will, so mote it be.

[this page intentionally left blank]

Free Gift

To thank you for purchasing this book, I'd like to give you a

100% FREE GIFT

Learn more about your free magickal gift.

Access Your Free Gift at
www.shamanschool.com

Find a complete list of magickal resources on https://amzn.to/3swxvPo. These resources are constantly updated so check back often!

Kitchen Table Relationship Magick
Table of Contents

[this page intentionally left blank]

Introduction to Kitchen Table Relationship Magick

"We're asking you to trust in the Well-being. In optimism there is magic."
~ Abraham

A Note About This Introduction

This book is one of a series of books in the Kitchen Table Magick series. Each book in the series addresses a specific area of magick (love, money, psychic development, etc.), and is written in a simple "recipe" format for people who want to use magick in their lives immediately. The Kitchen Table Magick series is akin to a Julia Childs recipe book, only these books contain magickal recipes for people to cook up some miraculous and magickal manifestations in their lives.

Because this series was designed so that each person could pick and choose to read just the books that pertain to their current life situation, each book is meant to be readable as a stand-alone book. To introduce the new reader to the series, this introduction to the series is repeated at the beginning of each book. If you have already read one or more books in this series, please feel free to jump ahead to the recipes that interest you. At the same time, some people feel that reviewing the introduction, as well as the "Rules and

1

Tips," is helpful before diving in. In magickal circles, your will is the guideline so choose whichever route best suits you... the Universe and magickal beings will follow!

What is Magick?

Many people have multiple different ideas about what magick is or can be. For the sake of clarity, here is what we know about magick after more than 35 years of study and practice. Magick is a precision science! It is also:

- The science of deliberate creation.
- The science of effective prayer.
- The science of manifesting Higher Will (substitute whatever Higher Force is most familiar to you) on the energetic and material planes.
- The science of heightened awareness, selective perception, and dynamic, harmonious relationships.
- The study of intention (as per Aleister Crowley, one of the greatest magickal practitioners in history).
- The system of creation, not coercion. Note: The word manipulation is often used in conjunction with magick, but manipulation simply means the use of the hands. It should be an "OK" word without a lot of charge, but currently it is used mostly to mean coercion. Look it up!
- The principle that every intentional act is a magickal act! Magick gives us the ability to communicate with beings on all levels, and allows us to understand, through direct experience, the actual workings of the Universe.
- The traditional path of spiritual growth.
- Not extraordinary knowledge. It is the "normal" way of life. We've just lost access to it. When you have this kind of knowledge in your understanding, you have the ability to resolve spiritual questions that otherwise become catechism. From a magickal point of view, catechism is not acceptable, since a practitioner must experience and verify everything for him or herself. It

avoids the trap of dogma. In past times, having a magickal foundation was essential so that we could talk directly to higher beings in the Universal hierarchy.

- Necessary to effective religious practice.

There is some confusion as to how to spell the word "magick." There are three different commonly used spellings: magick, magic, and majick. Eliphas Levi first used the form "magick" to differentiate religious or ceremonial from stage magick. All forms of spelling are acceptable in what this author teaches.

"I love Kitchen Table Magick! It's the best mix of both mystical and down-to-earth magick I have ever encountered. The fact that I can use items from my pantry is so handy and fun! It literally is about cooking up magic at my kitchen table, and having love show up in the least expected places!"
~ Wendy J., Skokie, IL

Is Magick Real?

Yes. Magick is very real and has existed as a precise science for thousands of years. Whether you use the word magick or another name, this spiritual practice is very real. Every single person can learn to do magick. We are ALL born with the talents and abilities that empower us to do magick. The only reason that magick seems so, well, magickal is that this society no longer teaches the art and science of magick. In the distant past, magickal study was just as important as math, science, or the arts. In fact, magick was and still is the birthright of EVERY planetary citizen.

Can you learn to do the kind of magick portrayed in the movies? Yes... and no. The movies are great at giving you a taste of what you can do with magick, but they are not very accurate. In the Harry Potter movies, for instance, the characters use their Wands for every magickal operation. In reality, you can only use the Wand to handle Air energies. Your Wand would actually explode or catch fire if you tried to use it to throw Firebolts and Fireballs as the characters do in the movie.

So, what can you actually do with magick? Quite a lot. Here is a short list to get you started:

- Balance your energies for healing and manifestation
- Change old beliefs
- Defend yourself against physical and psychic attack
- Heal yourself and others
- Find hidden information and see possible futures (and change the future if you do not like the probable futures you divine)
- Psychically communicate with other beings
- Create sacred space
- Find lost people and objects
- Manifest what you want and need in life

At the very basis of magick is the understanding of the four elements: Air, Fire, Water, and Earth. Called elemental magick, these foundational elements are real. Air, Fire, Water, and Earth are part of our natural everyday environment. What makes them magickal is the understanding of how they operate not just on the physical level, but also at the levels of Mind and Spirit.

For instance, while on the physical level, Air is just the stuff we breathe. On the magickal levels Air is the conduit of psychic communication, enlightenment, understanding, dreaming, and more. If you want more of these things in your life, then you need more magickal Air. How do you get more magickal Air? Wear more Air colors, including White for communication and Sky Blue for enlightenment and understanding. To take this one step further, you could also use various magickal techniques to take on more Air to make your body lighter. Take on enough Air and you'll be able to levitate.

By just extending your understanding and use of the

basic ingredients of nature, you are doing magick! Seen in this light, magick isn't all smoke and mirrors, nor is it the result of Hollywood special effects. Magick is the result of truly understanding and working with the very elements that are all around you.

One final note: Many masters, including Wayne Dyer, have said, "You'll see it when you believe it." The same is true for magick. In other words, the suspension of disbelief and the willingness not to exercise contempt prior to investigation are requirements for magick to be "real." Magick is all around us, and always is, but our ability to perceive and use the forces of magick depends on our willingness to be open. No one else can show it to you, only your direct experience and observation can "prove" or demonstrate to you that magick is real.

[this page intentionally left blank]

What is Kitchen Table Magick?

Kitchen Table Magick is exactly what it sounds like—a series of simple recipes that you can literally "cook up" at your kitchen table using household ingredients from your own pantry and cupboard.

The Kitchen Table Magick books have been created for ordinary people who want to mix up a little magick in their lives without all the fancy rituals, but simply with everyday ingredients that can be found in the kitchen pantry, bathroom medicine cabinet, or even stuffed in the back of the junk drawer.

The goal of these books is to allow anyone with the desire to learn this craft to mix up magick literally at the kitchen table using simple recipes. What goes into a simple recipe?

- Everyday items as ingredients
- Easy to follow instructions that don't require years of training
- Procedures that take less than two hours from start to finish
- Built-in expertise that allows the magick to do the heavy lifting
- Some friendly advice on how you can help your magickal recipe provide the best results
- Oh, and a few little rules and guidelines about magickal practice in this specific arena that will keep you safe and sound, magickally speaking, when you use these recipes

Kitchen Table Magick Equals:
Quick – Effective – Safe – Everyday Use – Ordinary
Affordable Ingredients

Why Use Kitchen Table Magic?

- Everyone can do magick.
- Magick should be simple, effective, and start working right away, else it is not magick.
- Not everyone has the time or resources to enroll in a school.
- People ask us for magickal help in hundreds of emails everyday... Kitchen Table Magick is designed to help these very people.
- Of the many areas of life, most people only seem to need help in one or two areas, so you need only buy those Kitchen Table Magick books that apply to your needs.
- Magick is for the masses, and should be accessible, affordable, and simple to do. This is what our teacher taught us, and this is the legacy we are paying forward as well.
- While there are many more advanced forms of magick, these books are an introduction to that world so that you can dabble, experiment, try things out, see the result, adjust and amend, and generally have fun... just as you would cooking a meal in your kitchen.
- This book is not for the major foodie, but is perfect for the person who needs magickal help right here, right now!

Who Should Use These Recipes?

- You and anyone you know who would like a little more magick and a little less ordinary reality in their lives.
- Anyone who needs help RIGHT now and doesn't have time to fly to India or Sedona to sit at the feet of a guru.

- Anyone who does not have access to anything but a computer for help and guidance.
- Anyone who wants to do magick and then forget it (all while quietly watching the magick "do its thing").
- Anyone who wants affordable, down to earth magick they can do with regular ingredients in the comfort of home.

When to Use Kitchen Table Magic: Anytime...
- You need help.
- You don't want to do all the heavy lifting (leave that to the Angels, Spirit Guides, Animal Totems, and so forth).
- You seem stuck in a rut or corner with no way out.
- You've been struggling with a problem for a long time and need a resolution.
- You don't know what to do but you need to do SOMETHING.
- You'd like to learn how to practice the craft.
- You want to live a more magickal life and stop dealing with ordinary hassles all the time.

How Do We Know These Recipes Work?
- We teach a slew of these recipes in one-day workshops all over the country, via teleconference, and via videoconference. We also email them to people as part of our school's service work, or post them on our blogs and articles library.
- We have used them for over 35 years and still do, every single day – literally tested out at our own kitchen tables for over 35 years (and at thousands of kitchen tables around the world) for a quarter century or more.
- We receive all kinds of stories and testimonials from happy successful students.

Kitchen Table Relationship Magick at Work...

Read the following example to discover how Psychic Magick works in real life...

Picture Perfect

The older I become it seems the more opinionated and set in my ways I am. Having lived through many years and all kinds of experiences, I found myself wanting a relationship, but unable to find a partner. While there were plenty of dates to be had, I couldn't seem to find the right partner who matched my standards, ethics, beliefs, or hobbies. When I tried speed dating, I was horrified! I met more people that I disliked at an even faster rate! Yuck!

Then I read the book on relationship magick. The information sounded really good... I felt that it was almost too good to be real. Flower essences and Spirit-to-Spirit communication were supposed to find me a mate? It didn't seem possible.

But I admit that I was desperate. Despite being

good at being alone, I still enjoyed the company of a partner. Finding one was a challenge. But the magickal tricks and tips I found in the relationship book intrigued me, so I wanted to check it out in the real world, to see if they really worked.

Long story short, I met a wonderful man who checked a lot of the boxes on my relationship list. As usual, though, there were problems. While we got along on most topics, actually making our relationship permanent included the challenge of creating a harmonious blended family, since both of us had children from previous marriages.

This was the perfect time to try out those relationship magick skills. The ones I ended up loving the most were the Chalice and Wand communication tools. Just as many proverbs say, when you have an idea that another person may or may not agree with, making it seem like the idea was theirs to begin with can make all the difference in the world.

With both Chalice and Wand communication, I was speaking to people in my new relationships not directly (especially on important issues where we disagreed), but rather I was planting seeds of thought via Spirit-to-Spirit and Mind-to-Mind communication without saying a single word out loud.

I was truly surprised when some of those seeds bore fruit. For instance, when it came to the wedding, I really wanted to have a down-home celebration that was fun, relaxed and joyful, as well as an outdoor ceremony that included our entire mixed family, from children to horses to in-laws. Nothing fancy, just fun.

My mate-to-be had other grander ideas. I didn't want that because I had already had the "big wedding" and the results were a mess. So, I diligently spent hours communicating my wishes, and the reasons behind those wishes, to everyone in our large extended family. At this point in my life, I was more interested in the personal relationships and less interested in putting on a big expensive affair. I just couldn't see pouring money down the drain like that and wanted the spend the same money on creating a happy homestead for our clan.

Lo and behold! My Wand and Chalice communications reached many naysayers in the family. We ultimately wed at a friend's ranch and had a wonderful celebration kicking up our bootheels under the open sky. The money we would have spent on a lavish wedding went toward building a sanctuary for our newly formed tribe.

With the experiences I gained from this wedding, I now constantly use my Chalice and Wand to communicate harmoniously with others when direct communication fails to do the trick. In truth, it seems that these techniques work because our Spirits are wiser than our practical selves, so agreement and harmony are more possible at the Spirit level than on the physical level. Amazing...
~ Maribel G., San Angelo, TX

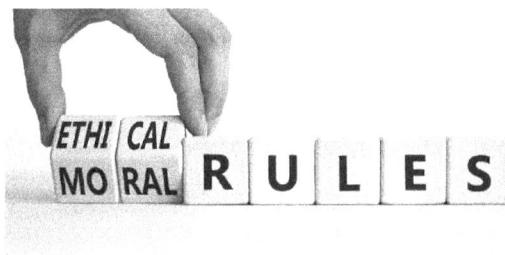

A Few Rules and Tips About Kitchen Table Magick

As with any game, the game of life has its own set of rules. Specifically, the spiritual side of life has rules. Play by those rules and you will stay safe and easily attract what you want into your life. Break those rules and all types of unwanted consequences happen.

These "spiritual rules" are ones that have been observed, both in personal spiritual practice and spiritual practice with various associated groups and teachers. These rules universally govern any spiritual practice, and appear to be in effect whether you know them or not. Unlike ethics and morals, which change with culture and time, these spiritual rules appear to have remained the same throughout time, unchanging, like physical and scientific rules.

The rules in the following section are adapted from *Rules of the Road*, as created by George Dew, co-founder of the Church of Seven Arrows. There are two major rules, which are common to most spiritual practices, along with some minor rules that are specific to our form of magickal practice.

Two Major Rules

These two rules will probably sound familiar, as they appear in most major religions and spiritual practices, most probably because they are common-sense and apply not just to spiritual practice, but to life as well.

First Rule: Golden Rule or Law of Karma
This first rule is literally a "golden oldie":

What you do to the environment or to other beings in the environment brings similar effects back to you in your life.

Often recognized as the Golden Rule or the Law of Karma, this rule tops the list because it reminds all spiritual practitioners of potential unwanted "rebound" or side effects. As your spiritual power, focus, and abilities grow, this rule will have an ever-greater impact on your life unless you exercise caution. The Universe responds more strongly and powerfully to those with focus, power, and ability.

Note: As humanity moves further in the Aquarian Age, many spiritual practitioners have seen more effects from this rule occur faster. In the past, effects of this rule that often took lifetimes to manifest now occur in minutes, days, weeks, or months. In this particular time in Earth's history, karma seems to operate under a "pay as you go" system. Simply stated, expect the effects of the Law of Karma to occur quickly.

Second Rule: The Judgment of "Good and Bad" According to the Universe
This second rule adds clarity and detail to the first rule described previously:

If you are unsure whether your acts are "good or bad"-- that is, whether those acts are in keeping with universal laws on this planet—the Universe will reflect its judgment back to you quickly, according to the "pay as you go" Law of Karma.

This law holds as true for individuals as it does for entire communities, states, nations, or other organized groups. If you are still unsure of the feedback you receive from the Universe, check areas such as your level of health, the soundness of social relationships, your prosperity or lack of, sufficiency of various needs in life, and even your "luck" with appliances and machines. If your luck appears to be consistently poor, then you are probably acting contrary to universal governing laws, regardless of your intentions. The Universe cares about what you do more than what you intend.

Additional Detailed Rules

The following rules offer more detailed standards by which to measure your acts or the acts of others to determine whether these acts are in accordance with universal laws.

- Do nothing that will harm another being unless you are willing to suffer similar or greater harm. What the Universe considers "harm" may be different than what you consider harm.
- Do not bind another being unless you are willing to be similarly bound. An example of binding someone is doing acts in attempt to coerce a specific other person to love you. There is no problem with attracting your soul mate into your life, but doing acts that attempt to coerce a specific other person to love you is a type of binding.
- Never use your spiritual abilities in vain, to show off, or to boost your pride. Using your spiritual abilities from a place of pride usually causes the Universe to bring instant backlash into your life.
- If you choose to charge money or barter for using your spiritual abilities in the service of others, avoid charging extremely high prices. Charge prices for using methods comparable to other professionals, such as an attorney or accountant.
- Never use any spiritual word, chant, litany, or similar "device" unless you are confident in your understanding of its methods, intents, and effects.
- When undertaking a major spiritual operation—one that will require significant effort or attempts to create a major effect in the world—use divination to

determine whether you can safely benefit from such an operation, and to discover the obstacles you must overcome. Divination methods such as pendulum readings, channeling, meditation, and question circles (to name a few) can reveal hidden factors of which you may be unaware.

- In any spiritual endeavor, take your time, think it through, and do it right!

The good news is that you can still do relationship magick rituals. The ones we teach in this book won't get you in trouble with the Universe while also allowing you to attract the relationships you want, strengthening the ones you have, and letting go the ones you no longer need in your life.

The Ingredients of Relationship Magick

"The purpose of a relationship is not to have another who might complete you, but to have another with whom you might share your completeness."
~ Neale Donald Walsch

Relationships between people can be tricky and complicated and can blur boundaries. When using magick to work on relationship issues there are two principles that are important to remember. These are that magickally speaking you have the right to your own sacred space, and you must be careful not to bind another person.

The Rules of the Road, which are the set of Universal ethics and must be followed for safe and effective magickal practice. These rules are not the same as morals (what our culture teaches us is right and wrong) or ethics (what we personally believe to be right and wrong), as both morals and ethics change over time, are particularly applicable in relationship magick. You will find a complete list and explanation of these at the front of this ebook under the section entitled *"A Few Rules and Tips About Kitchen Table Magick"*. In general, the ones that need to be specifically kept in mind when engaging in relationship magick include:

- What you do to the environment or to other beings in the environment brings similar effects back to you in your life.
- Do nothing that will harm another being unless you are willing to suffer similar or greater harm. What the Universe considers "harm" may be different than what you consider harm.
- Do not bind another being unless you are willing to be similarly bound. An example of binding someone is doing acts in attempt to coerce a specific other person to love you. There is no problem with attracting your soul mate into your life, but doing acts that attempt to coerce a specific other person to love you is a type of binding.
- Never use your spiritual abilities in vain, to show off, or to boost your pride. Using your spiritual abilities from a place of pride usually causes the Universe to bring instant backlash into your life.

In some cases, the rules that govern self-defense magick can also be applicable to relationships and using relationship magick. Before engaging in any magickal procedure that could be in response to you being treated poorly or injured emotionally, physically, or mentally, be sure you are adhering to the laws that govern the use of self-defense magick:

"In cases of direct and violent personal harm you are entitled to defend yourself by any means available provided you did nothing to encourage or provoke the attack."

Direct – Means upon body, mind, or spirit. A direct threat in spiritual, magickal, and shamanic definitions includes attempts by any outside force or influence to drain your energy or impose their will upon you.

Violent – Means anything that is damaging to your

physical, mental, emotional, or spiritual well-being. Doesn't matter what the other person's intentions are, only what they does.

Encourage – Means creating or permitting unnecessary opportunities for a known hostile being to attack you.

Provoke – Means being overly pushy when you know someone has a particularly sensitive area or is under a lot of stress whether it be internal or external.

By Any Means Available – Means using any means that you choose to defend yourself when attacked. If all the other conditions of this rule are met, the Universe does not judge whether your response is excessive.

[this page intentionally left blank]

Relationship Magick Appetizer Recipes

Appetizers: Broaden Your Relationship Choices

Flower Essences

Exercising Choice

"Compromise has frequently been difficult for me, which tends to explain why I have had so few relationships. But after creating some relationship flower essences, and practicing the art of conscious choice, I find that I am much more flexible with other people. You could say that my heart was bigger and more open. Also, with these two little rituals I have never felt 'trapped' in a relationship. It's as if these rituals are open doorways to every relationship— some doors lead to deeper connection while other ones lead to freedom from a certain relationship."
~ Violet M., Redwood City, CA

[this page intentionally left blank]

Flower Essences

"Let us be grateful to the people who make us happy; they are the charming gardeners who make our souls blossom."
~ Marcel Proust

Time Required: Sixty Minutes

Flower essences use the natural healing properties of flowering plants to create healing effects primarily in the subtle or non-physical bodies. This can include the auric, mental, and emotional bodies. Flower essences work well for emotional upheavals, spiritual disconnection, depression, recurring life issues, mental distress, all of which can affect relationships. This recipe will give you the directions for making your own flower essences which is a peaceful and refreshing way to reconnect yourself with the Nature around you and can enhance the relationship you are working on especially if you and the other person work on the essences together.

Ingredients

- Tweezers
- Distilled water
- Clear glass bowl
- Alcohol (80 proof vodka) or organic, unfiltered, apple cider vinegar
- Quart size cobalt or brown jar
- Several 1-2 ounce brown dropper bottles

Recipe Directions

1. Decide on the flower essence you will make and find the plant. (See the list at the end of this recipe for some ideas of flower essences to use in relationships).

2. Communicate with the plant first by sitting quietly by the plant, breathing deeply, and opening yourself and your heart. Be in silence and ask the plant Deva for permission to use the plant's blossoms for healing. Speak to the plant the same way you would to anyone, but even more gently. You can either speak out loud or project your thoughts toward the plant. Wait until you hear a response.

3. Say to the plant Deva, "Please infuse this water with your divine essence." You can also leave an offering at the base of the plant so that there is an even exchange of giving and receiving energy. Appropriate offerings can include beautiful rocks, consecrated tobacco or cornmeal, or a strand of your own hair.

4. Pour the distilled water into the glass bowl.

5. Use the tweezers to gently remove each blossom at its base and respectfully place it in the water. Another method suggests bending the stem of the plant so that the blossom rests in the water, but not to remove the blossom itself. This method is thought to preserve the

integrity of the plant. If you use the blossoms, follow your intuition as to how many and choose only those that are in their prime or just coming into their prime.

6. Place the bowl with water and blossoms or petals in the sun or leave it sitting at the base of the plant for 1-4 hours. Again, use your intuition for the amount of time. Also pick the time of day to make the essence depending on the type of energy you want for your essence. For example, dawn energy is good for initiating or beginning energy.

7. Remember throughout the process to remain quietly peaceful, not in a hurry and don't allow your actions to become mechanical. This is a process of communing with nature.

8. Next add alcohol to the mixture to prevent external bacteria from contaminating your essence. The mixture should be 50% alcohol and 50% water. Add the water into the cobalt or brown glass jar, then add the alcohol. This mixture is the "mother tincture". The brown or cobalt glass protects the tincture against light which has its own vibration and can cause the tincture to decompose.

9. Store the mother tincture in a cool, dark place such as a dark closest, freezer, or root cellar.

10. When ready to make your actual flower essence, fill a small brown dropper bottle with distilled water and add one dropper full of the mother tincture to it. Succuss the water by striking the bottom of the bottle on the palm of your hand about 50 times. This mixes the mother tincture with the water and excites the molecules.

How to Use the Results of Your Recipe

Be sure when using flower essences to do some research on which one or ones will be most helpful for your situation and find out if each is safe to take as a tincture or should only be used as aromatherapy. Some of the flower essences that you may find useful in dealing with relationship issues include:

- Chamomile - nervousness, anxiety.
  - Gift: calming, relaxing.
- Mimulus - long time fears, extremes, dominated.
  - Gift: fearless, confident.
- Cherry Plum - loss of control, vicious, to remain in control.
  - Gift: calm, quiet, in control.
- Red Chestnut - worry.
  - Gift: positive, calm.
- Willow - resentment.
  - Gift: optimistic, responsible, acceptance.
- Sweet Chestnut - despairing, burned out.
  - Gift: faith, trust.
- Pine - rejection, abuse, guilt, never succeeding.
  - Gift: responsible, humble.
- Oak - chronic exhaustion, overworked but keeps struggling.
  - Gift: strong, dependable.
- Star of Bethlehem - any kind of trauma or loss of a loved one, gives comfort.
  - Gift: comforts all traumas.
- Gorse - hopelessness, giving up.
  - Gift: faith, hope, positive.
- Gentian - setbacks, disappointment.
  - Gift: restores hope, long illness rehabilitation.
- Heather - needing attention.
  - Gift: vital, selfless.
- Wild Rose - to remain happy and content.
  - Gift: joy, contentment, accepting.

- Beech -intolerance.
  - Gift: tolerance, acceptance.
- Jasmine - anxiety, dilemmas that deal with relationships.
  - Gift: confidence, energy, optimism, increase feeling of attractiveness.
- Ylang Ylang - sex drive problems, frustration, impotence.
  - Gift: influences sexual energy, enhances relationships, balance male-female energies.

[this page intentionally left blank]

Exercising Choice

"May your choices reflect your hopes, not your fears."
~ Nelson Mandela

Time Required: Ten Minutes Per Day

Sometimes you have a choice to make when it comes to a relationship. Is this a relationship you want to continue, or does it no longer serve you or is no longer an energetic match for you and it is time to end it? Are you unsatisfied with your current relationships and want to increase the level of your being to raise the level of those you attract to yourself?

Knowing your partner in a relationship is not going to change and accepting that you cannot change them leaves you with the decision to either accept that person as they are or end that relationship. Sometimes though, when you increase the level of your being, the other person just drifts away from you because you no longer match. This recipe will help you become more solid in making these hard decisions based on listening to your inner knowing and help you increase your consciousness thus raising the level of your own being.

Ingredients

- Desire to increase relationship with higher powers and beings
- Willingness to do this exercise each day consistently
- Way to keep track of the number of days in a row you have done the exercise

Recipe Directions

1. Either out loud or silently, say to yourself, "I will now make a conscious choice."

2. Ask yourself a choice question now. "Do I choose to do this or that?" (i.e., relax and read a book or go for a walk.) The question might also be "What do I choose to do right now?"

3. Take a moment to be silent and listen to your inner self. The first answer that comes to you is what you must do. Make sure if you are in a place or time where you cannot do certain things that you do not make those things part of the choice. For example, if you are at work and would get in trouble for sleeping on the job, don't make one of the choices "go take a nap".

4. Do this exercise each day for 40 days. If you miss a day, and you most certainly will, start over at Day 1. Don't beat yourself up for starting over. This is part of the journey and the primary goal is having the practice, not getting to the 40 day goal.

How to Use the Results of Your Recipe

We say start with trivial choices because you are just learning to listen to and trust your inner guidance. In that process it really won't matter too much if you have oatmeal instead of eggs for breakfast. However, by practicing with these small, less important choices, you'll be able to develop your inner voice and learn to trust your own inner wisdom. That way when bigger life choices such as whether to continue a relationship or not come along, you'll have the experience of accessing your own inner wisdom as well as the consistent relationship with the Universe to draw on for help in making the right decisions for you.

[this page intentionally left blank]

Relationship Magick Main Course Recipes

Main Courses: Saying What You Need to Say in Relationships

Chalice Communication

Cutting Unhealthy Psychic Lines

Wand Communication

"Sometimes saying what you really feel in a relationship can be very hard, especially if you fear how the other person is going to react. This can apply to every relationship, from family and friends, to co-workers and neighbors. I love using the Chalice and Wand to communicate because it helps me reach the heart and mind of the person to whom I'm speaking. It's all done through Spirit-to-Spirit or Mind-to-Mind communication, so the fallout is rarely a big deal. My relationships have made a quantum leap since I started using the Chalice and Wand!"
~ Chamberlain L., Springfield, MO

[this page intentionally left blank]

Chalice Communication

"When you don't talk, there's a lot of stuff that ends up not getting said."
~ Catherine Gilbert Murdock

Time Required: Thirty Minutes

Sometimes your relationship is suffering due to a lack of communication. Whether you are afraid of talking about a certain subject that makes you feel uncomfortably vulnerable or are afraid of how another person will react or just want to avoid a messy confrontation, using the Water element tool, Chalice, can help you communicate with another person on a Spirit-to-Spirit level.

Since the Water element is associated with emotions, this form of communication is particularly good for reaching out to someone on an emotional level. You must first obtain a Chalice and as you do with most magickal tools, key it. Keying your Chalice allows you to clear out any impure energy, personalize it to you and align the molecules for the energy to flow in a particular direction. There is a more permanent form of keying a Chalice, but for this recipe we will give you a quick keying method to use.

Ingredients

- Chalice that is a goblet shaped cup with a stem, made of either glass or ceramic, Water Blue or Clear in color and is either smooth or patterned if the pattern is not too deep
- Water Blue color source (mid color between light and dark blue)
- Dark, flat liquid
- Flat surface such as a table to set Chalice on

Recipe Directions

1. To key your Chalice, cup your hands on either side of the bowl part of the Chalice, use your Water Blue color source to pull energy from and begin circling Water Blue energy from your output hand (hand you point with) through the Chalice into your input hand, up your input arm, across your shoulders down your output arm and out your output hand again. Circulate the color Water Blue for approximately 3 minutes, then pull your water energy back in and your Chalice is keyed temporarily.

2. Fill the Chalice with a dark flat liquid such as coffee or flat soda, leaving ½-¾ inches headspace at the top of the Chalice.

3. Sit in the South facing North, place your Chalice in front of you and block out all distractions.

4. Move the Chalice so that you are looking at the liquid's surface at a 45 degree angle.

5. Visualize the face of the person you want to communicate with just under the surface of the dark

liquid to establish a direct psycho-spiritual link with them.

6. Start talking to them just as you would as if they were physically present. Make sure your attention is focused on that person, your message, and any responses that come and not on any other thoughts or anything that distracts your attention. Become very emotionally interested and curious about the communication as that can help carry the message across more strongly.

7. If you notice the surface of the dark liquid becomes steamy or cloudy or start to get a headache or achy eyes, you are pushing too hard. Relax, breathe, and try to continue talking to the person just like you would in person. Some people find closing their eyes works better for them.

How to Use the Results of Your Recipe

Communicating from your Spirit to another's Spirit can help you understand what is really going on with your partner which could be something they are aware of and just scared to talk about or could be something they are not even consciously aware of. This form of communication can help you avoid messy interactions that may not turn out well or it can just be a way to open up and facilitate an in-person conversation. If you are just sending a message to someone such as your boss's spirit, then you are done once you go through the recipe steps. But if you are having a true conversation, you'll need to wait for a response. Since this is a communication from Spirit, the answer may be in a different form than the person would usually give from their everyday personality. Be aware of what messages you hear in your head or that come to you from your surroundings. You may also need to do this communication more than once to increase its effectiveness.

Chalice messages affect the emotions and can be very

strong and become quite compulsive, so you should make sure you are following Rules of the Road (at the intro to this ebook) when sending these types of messages. The Rules of the Road say not to bind anyone. So if you send a compulsive type message, you are breaking this rule. For example, if you were to tell your co-worker you want to avoid "Stay home", they may not be able to leave their house at all for any reason which could be dangerous. It is better to remember this form of communication is not for you to give commands but to facilitate communication and understanding.

Cutting Unhealthy Psychic Lines

"Just say NO to complicated, dead-end, unhealthy, and toxic relationships."
~ Stephanie Lahart

Time Required: Sixty Minutes

Using an Athame (Fire element tool) to project a fire energy beam, you can cut psychic lines to release unhealthy relationships and situations by severing the psychic attachment they have to you. Cutting lines on a person will not affect healthy relationships or situations, only unhealthy ones. Much of the time these lines are not established through conscious intention but by forces such as worrying about another person, grieving over a relationship that has ended, or being jealous of another person. If your relationship is suffering from any type of unhealthy attachment from another person that is keeping you bound to them for any reason, or there are negative energies being directed towards your relationship such as from others who disapprove or are jealous, then this recipe can help you deal with those issues magickally.

You can cut lines on your partner and have your partner cut lines on you. If you just need to separate from an unhealthy relationship and can't seem to get the other person to disengage, then you can cut lines on yourself either using a simulacrum of yourself and the Athame or with a Plate (Earth element tool). We will present you with both techniques in this recipe.

Ingredients

- A keyed Athame, Fire element tool
- When selecting an Athame to use as a magick tool, look for a knife with a single-edged blade that is straight, not curved, made from high carbon, nickel alloy or chrome alloy steel and that has a full tang which means the steel goes all the way through the handle or mostly all the way through and it should not be a folding knife
- Once you have selected your Athame, it needs to be keyed to personalize it to your particular energies. Do this by lining up the molecules for energy to flow from base to tip and clear out negative energies. There is a very specific procedure to follow to permanently "key" your Athame, but to just use this one recipe, you can do an "emergency keying" by pointing the tip of the knife towards the North, and then striking the butt of the handle forcefully with anything hard, such as an iron skillet or a stone. This will keep it keyed for between 15 minutes to a day
- An Electric Blue color source (can be candle flame or square of colored paper)
- Knowledge of directions or a compass to help you locate cardinal directions (North, South, East, West)
- Diagram below showing where you will make cuts (black dot represents other person)

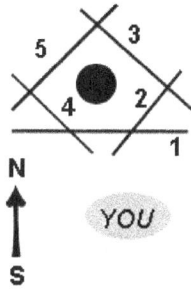

- An open space, 5-10 feet in diameter, in which you can set up your circle
- A round plate 6-10 inches in diameter, made of wood, ceramic or porcelain, glass or metal that is of earth tone colors or has plant-based designs in earth tones and doesn't have deeply carved patterns. You should be able to hold it easily by placing your thumbs in the center and the rest of your fingers on the edge
- Firebowl made of brass, cast-iron, ceramic or a hard hardwood that is 4-6 inches in diameter and 4-5 inches deep that can be easily held with one or both hands and light enough to carry in one hand if necessary. Make sure it will be stable when placed on a flat surface and that the shape of the bowl is curved-in and flared back out at the top rim to promote "columning" of incense or smoke. (Fill with fine sand or ground fire clay and self-starting charcoal disks on top of that, and water element incense such as gardenia, rose, lotus blossom, or strawberry to burn on the charcoal disk)
- Paper or wooden matches
- Chalice and spring water and sea salt to charge it
- Pure cotton cloth
- Earth Brown color source and Electric Blue color source (optional with Plate)

Recipe Directions (Athame technique)

1. Stand in the South facing North and have the person you are cutting lines on stand to the North of you

facing away from you and several feet away from you.

2. Have the person close their eyes and ask them to relax.

3. Load your Athame with the Fire energy color of Electric Blue from your color source and project a beam of Electric Blue off the tip of your Athame 3-5 feet beyond the person. This beam will be used to cut through the lines. Do this by "pulling" the color from your color source using your input hand (opposite hand from the one you naturally point with), run it up your arm, across your shoulders, down your other arm into the hand holding the Athame (output hand) and into the Athame itself. Don't overthink this process, just feel yourself pulling the energy in and out into the Athame, projecting the beam off its tip.

4. Standing at a right angle to the person several feet away from them, make the first cut directly behind them by starting with aiming the beam at a level above their head and making a forceful downward cut. The beam should be about a foot away from the person's back. Understand that you are using the beam of energy you are projecting off the blade of the Athame to cut the psychic lines around the person's physical body. At no time does the actual Athame itself touch the person's body and you are in fact several feet away from the other person.

5. The 2nd cut is made to the right and slightly behind the person in the same way as the first.

6. The 3rd cut is made to the person's right again, but closer to the front side of their body (Do not make the cut directly in front of them).

7. The next two cuts are made to the left side of the

person's body, reflecting the two positions of the cuts you made to the right side.

8. Finally, make a horizontal cut above the person's head from right to left, and below the person's feet (you can extend your beam into the floor to make this cut). The blade edge of the Athame faces left as you make these two cuts.

9. To cut lines on yourself, you will do the same procedure as described here on a simulacrum keyed to yourself. A simulacrum in this instance will need to be some type of doll or figurine or statue that you can key to represent you. For the purpose of cutting lines, the simulacrum must be something you can stand up so in this case using just a picture of yourself would not work. However, you can paste a picture of your face on the figurine if you wish but it is not necessary.

10. You will key the figurine or doll to your own energies by holding it in your dominant or "output" hand (hand you naturally point with) and thinking of everything you know about yourself, flowing that energy and those thoughts into the figurine. Continue this until it feels charged, warm, heavy or tingly, or you get the feeling that the simulacrum is "alive" or feel it wiggle. After the simulacrum is keyed, you must be very careful with it. Whatever happens to it will happen to the person or thing it is keyed to, which in this case is yourself.

11. When you have finished cutting your lines using the simulacrum you will need to "unkey" it from being a representation of yourself. You have just cut lines using the simulacrum which means you have cut those unhealthy attachments to yourself that exist. Now you will once again cut lines with your Athame on the simulacrum, this time with the intention of

cutting the psychic connection lines that exist between yourself and the simulacrum. Then throw a blast of Electric Blue energy at it from your Athame to complete the unkeying.

Recipe Directions (Plate technique)

1. These first 9 steps will guide you in keying your Plate to clear out any impure energy, align all the molecules so the energy flows in a particular direction and to personalize the Plate to your own energies. To begin, gather your Firebowl, Chalice (see directions on selecting in previous recipe on Chalice Communication), materials needed to charge both, and a pure cotton cloth.

2. Feel the energy of your Plate before you begin by moving your palm back and forth above it.

3. Sit in the South facing North and charge your Firebowl (see next recipe #6b if you need a refresher on how to charge Firebowl) and Chalice (with spring water and a pinch of sea salt in it) using the verse:

   "Water and Earth where you are cast,
   Let no spell nor adverse purpose last,
   Not in accord with me!
   Cleanse these tools and cleanse its space,
   Far from here send baneful trace!
   Thus my will, so it be!"

   Use a water or general-purpose incense in your Firebowl instead of sage and pine resin.

4. Hold your Plate upside down (dished side down) in the column of smoke from the Firebowl. Allow the smoke to drift onto the Plate for 15-30 seconds. If the Plate has been previously used by other people or for another purpose, it may take more time for the smoke

to clear out the energies. Pull the Plate away from the smoke and see if the smoke sticks to it (little streamers of smoke will billow off the Plate if the smoke is sticking). If not, put the Plate back over the Firebowl until the smoke sticks.

5. Smoke the bottom of your Plate in the same way until the smoke sticks.

6. Dip a corner of your cotton cloth into the water of your Chalice. Use the wet area of the cloth to wipe the top of the plate (the concave side). Start at the center of the Plate and begin wiping clockwise, moving your cloth outward in a spiral. Wipe with pressure and intention until the top of the Plate has been wiped.

7. Without stopping or lifting the cotton cloth from the plate continue wiping by moving to the rim of the Plate, then turn the Plate over and continue wiping the back of the Plate in the same direction. Do not change directions once you reach the back – the wiping should be in one smooth continuous stroke. When you turn the Plate over you will be wiping in a counter-clockwise direction. You may want to have another person watch you to ensure that you do not change directions. If you change directions when you start wiping the back, your Plate may actually split in half during intense magickal operations. You could end up with two very thin but completely round plates.

8. Using a dry corner of your cotton cloth repeat the wiping procedure remembering to wipe with steady pressure and intention.

9. Test the energy of your Plate again and notice any differences.

10. Stand in an open space where you can easily turn all the way around with your arm extended out in front of you.

11. There are two ways to position your hands and your Plate:
    - Hold the Plate in your output hand (hand you point with) with your output arm slightly extended at chest height. Hold your input hand with palm facing away from you behind the center of the Plate. The front of the Plate should face away from you. OR
    - Hold the Plate in your input hand with your input arm slightly extended at chest height. Hold your output hand with palm facing you in front of the center of the Plate. The front of the Plate should face away from you.

12. Turn in a clockwise circle always facing the outside of the circle (you can make the circle as big as 6-10 feet in diameter), feeling for hot and cold spots that show up in the center of the Plate with whichever hand is not holding the Plate.
    - If you feel a cold spot, someone is pulling energy from you. We call these people psychic vampires.
    - If you feel a hot spot, someone is pushing on you, exerting some control over you or adding their energy to yours.

13. Stop when you feel a hot or cold spot. There are four different ways to disconnect the lines, each with an increasing amount of force:
    - Scatter the Energies: This approach has the least amount of force, and simply breaks the line without causing it to snap back to the sender. Simply turn your Plate so that the front faces you, with your thumbs in the center and the rest of your fingers on the edges. Hold your Plate in this

position in the center of the hot or cold spot (which indicates a line) for a few seconds to disconnect the line.

- Snap the Line: This approach cuts the line and snaps it back to the sender with a little force, so that the sender gets a little jolt. Hold your Plate so that the front faces away from you, with your thumbs in the center and the rest of your fingers on the edges. Give a little push with your Plate to snap the line. If you snap a line on someone who is pulling or pushing very hard it could give them a jolt and knock them out when it snaps back on them.

- Send Brown: Follow the same procedure as for snapping the line. Before you push with your Plate, though, load a little Earth Brown into your Plate by pulling it in through your elbows and when you push with your Plate send a little Earth Brown down the line. The Earth Brown energy will produce a bigger jolt and will act as a warning to the sender to leave you alone.

- Send a Lemniscate: If the line feels really heavy or if it feels like the person is really doing something harmful to you, you can draw an Electric Blue Lemniscate with your finger or your Athame and push that down the line with your Plate. This will push or pull on the sender with as much force as they were pushing or pulling on the line. The Lemniscate will not release them until they let go completely. The Lemniscate could tie the person up for the rest of their life unless they let go! (A Lemniscate is like a figure 8 turned on its side - ∞.

14. Continue around the circle until you have cut all the lines at chest height. You may then want to repeat the procedure holding your plate head high and waist high.

How to Use the Results of Your Recipe

When cutting lines with an Athame, be sure to hold the Athame tightly with both hands so that it does not bounce off a tough line. Make sure as you make the various cuts that you overlap them so you get all the lines on every side. Don't cut directly in front of a person as they have a lot of shielding in the front of the body. Some people notice that they are a bit dizzy or feel tired after this procedure has been done. They may need to sit for a while or rest and you may want to sweep them with a flare of Sun Yellow energy off the Athame from head to feet to add back energy.

To cut lines on another person with the Plate, have them stand in the center of the room with their eyes closed. Start at their back (so that you are back-to-back with the person) and walk around them, always facing the outside of the circle, staying as close to the other person as you can. Use your Plate in the same manner as if you were cutting lines on yourself.

Wand Communication

"Communication is the fuel that keeps the fire of your relationship burning, without it, your relationship goes cold."
~ William Paisley

Time Required: Sixty Minutes

Often relationship problems are due to a lack of good communication. If you find this to be the case and need a little magickal help getting your point across or facilitating communication between yourself and another person, this recipe can help. Wand messages act on the mind or consciousness of the recipient and usually appear in the form of a sudden thought. The Wand is the Air element tool, and you will need to make your own wand in order to use this recipe. Be sure you never push any energies other than Air energies (White, Clear, or Sky Blue) through your Wand. These are the only energies the Wand is designed to conduct safely.

The first 6 steps in the Recipe Directions give you the

instructions for making and keying your Wand. The rest of the directions are specifically on how to send messages using your Wand. Refer to the recipe previously given on Cutting Unhealthy Psychic Lines if you need reminding how to select and use the Firebowl as you will need this in keying the Wand.

Ingredients
- A fairly straight limb that is ¼-⅜ inch diameter from a live tree or recently fallen from a live tree, is light-weight and light colored, and is no longer than from the bend of your elbow to the tip of your middle finger. (White pine, birch, peeled willow, or aspen are examples of good Air-oriented woods)
- Small knife to peel off bark and carve
- Fine sandpaper
- Charged Firebowl and the charcoal disk, wood shavings, pine resin, and sage to burn in it
- Sun Yellow candle
- Wooden or paper matches
- White, Clear, and/or Sky Blue color sources (can be squares of colored paper)
- Knowledge of direction East or compass to find it

Recipe Directions
1. Select your limb as described above by taking a walk in an area with trees. If you take the limb from a live tree, be sure to ask permission of the tree first. Your Wand is an important magickal tool and should be personal to you so take your time in selecting one that draws you to it.

2. Use a small knife to peel the bark off the limb.

3. Use your fine sandpaper to go over the limb and make it smooth to the touch.

4. Once all the bark is removed and it is smooth, carve a notch at the end of the limb that was closest to the trunk of the tree. Carve a large, open notch in this base end to allow your wand to easily draw in Air energies. The notch will resemble a "V" shape.

5. Now use your knife to whittle a slightly rounded point on the growing end of the limb (opposite end from the notch). This will be the tip of the Wand.

6. You will now "key" your Wand to your own energies to make it uniquely your own and to align the molecules in the tool so that the energies flow in a certain direction. To key your Wand:

   a. First feel the energetic quality of your Wand by running your hands over it or holding it 1-2 inches above your arm and sweeping it up and down. Remember how your Wand feels before it is keyed.

   b. Stand in the South facing North and charge your Firebowl by lighting the Sun candle with paper or wooden matches, then lighting another match from the candle to light the charcoal disk in the Firebowl. Once the charcoal disk in your Firebowl is lit, pull Sun Yellow energy from your candle into yourself and blow it out onto the disk. Add pine resin and sage to the lit charcoal and in a voice of command, say out loud:

      "Fire and Air where you are cast,
      Let no spell nor adverse purpose last,
      Not in accord with me!
      Cleanse this tool and cleanse its space,
      Far from here send baneful trace!
      Thus my will, so it be!"

   c. Once the Firebowl is sending up a thick column of

smoke, hold your Wand in the middle of the smoke column with the tip pointing North and the base (the notched end) towards you.

d. Start pulling the Wand through the smoke toward you with the notch end entering the smoke first. Hold the Wand an inch above the rim of the Firebowl.

e. Keep pulling the Wand slowly and deliberately through the smoke, rolling it a little as you pull it through. Look for the smoke to stick to the Wand.

f. Once the smoke sticks to the entire length of the Wand, hold it vertically in the column of smoke, notch end down, about an inch from the charcoal.

g. With your intention, pull the smoke up along the entire length of the Wand until it covers the entire Wand and floats off the tip. This step aligns the molecules in your Wand so that energies move from base to tip only. This protects you from any energies coming back at you.

h. Feel your Wand again. It should feel different to you now that it has been keyed. If you do not feel the difference, repeat the process with the Firebowl.

7. Decide whether you want to use White, Clear, or Sky Blue, and have your color source ready. White or Sky Blue tend to be more effective than Clear. White acts on the mind and Sky Blue acts on the spiritual level. If the person is very busy mentally you may want to choose Sky Blue so you won't have to compete with all of the person's White energy. Send your message when the person is likely to be mentally or spiritually available (i.e., not in the middle of a busy meeting).

8. Face East, and hold your Wand in your output hand (hand you naturally point with). Hold the notched end in the hollow of your hand and put your first two fingers and thumb around the Wand. Cock the elbow of your output hand so it is at a 90 degree angle to the ground, arm extended out from the shoulder so the Wand is pointing straight up.

9. Pull in the Air color you want to use with your input hand, then look at your Wand. Take three breaths and really push the color into your Wand with each breath. The Wand may quiver as you push energy into it.

10. Turn in the direction of your output hand and see the person's face you wish to send a message to beyond your arm.

11. Straighten your arm, palm up and shoot the energies out of the Wand at the "mock up" of the person's face with an outward breath. At the same time, say your message in a voice of command (strong voice). Be sure your palm is up! If you send a message with palm down the energies shoot out of the Wand with laser beam force. This may overwhelm the person with Air energies and make them too distracted or "spaced out" to understand your message. Remember, too, that if you make a person distracted and they get into trouble as a result, the Universe will hold you accountable!

How to Use the Results of Your Recipe

Since Air is a lightweight element, it is a good choice for facilitating communication because it doesn't have much force so you can't command anyone to do anything which keeps you on the right side of Universal Rules of the Road. You can send an idea, but the recipient is still able to decide whether to act on that idea or not. Short messages, like "Call me" or "I love you" seem to work the best with Wand messages. To increase the effectiveness of your message, send it more than once at different times of the day or try sending it in different colors. The person may get the message but not know who sent it or they may get the idea but be too busy to act on it.

Relationship Magick Dessert Recipes

Desserts: Relationship Harmony Through Ritual

Nighttime Blessing Ritual

Question Circle for Guidance

"Bringing a blended family together isn't the easiest thing in the world, especially if the children are young, and custody issues get in the way. One of my family's most favorite things to create harmony is the nighttime blessing ritual. Somehow this simple but intentional ritual helps everyone get in tune with the current members of the family, and the kids are really proud to take part in this ritual. It makes them feel really grown-up and very happy!"
~ Jolene E., Kalamazoo, MI

[this page intentionally left blank]

Nighttime Blessing Ritual

"Some people come in our life as blessings. Some come in your life as lessons."
~ Mother Teresa

Time Required: Ten Minutes Per Day

The ritual in this recipe is a great way to improve harmony and connection between you and your partner using the Water element tool, the Chalice. Done at night just before bed for 40 nights in a row, it can make magickal changes in your relationship with your significant other. It can also be done with the whole family, yourself alone, or with your pets.

Ingredients
- A Chalice that is a goblet shaped cup with a stem, made of either glass or ceramic, Water Blue or Clear in color and that is either smooth or has a pattern that

is not too deep
- Water Blue color source
- Sea salt
- Spring water

Recipe Directions

1. Holding the Chalice with both hands in front of you, flow Water Blue energy you pull from your color source, from one hand to the other, through the Chalice. Continue until the Chalice becomes warm or tingly. This "keys" the Chalice to the person holding it.

2. Pour spring water into the Chalice until it is halfway full and add a pinch of sea salt to it. Swirl the mixture in the Chalice in a clockwise direction.

3. Blow Water Blue energy into the Chalice while swirling the water and salt mixture clockwise. In between each time you blow energy in, say one line of the verse below:

   "Water and Earth where you are cast,
   Let no spell nor adverse purpose last.
   Bless these people and bless their space,
   Far from here send baneful trace."

4. At the end of the verses, blow Water Blue energy into the Chalice and swirl the water one last time. The Chalice is now "charged."

5. Holding the Chalice in your left hand, face your partner whom you will be blessing. Dip your right index finger into the water and draw a vertical line down the center of his or her forehead. The line should be 1-1.5 inches long.

6. Now dip your finger in the water again and draw a horizontal line of the same length from left to right

through the center of the first line, forming a cross.

7. Then, starting at the right end of the horizontal line, draw a clockwise circle, touching both ends of both lines. As you draw the circle and say your partner, "For the peace of your mind."

8. Repeat the same procedure on your partner's chest over their heart. As you draw the circle, say, "For the joy of your heart."

9. Ask your partner to take a sip of water from the Chalice and as they sip, say, "And for the health of your body."

10. Now, reverse roles and have your partner repeat the process on you.

How to Use the Results of Your Recipe

This doesn't have to be saved for night, but many people, couples, and families like ending the day with this ritual each night before bedtime. It is a great ritual to incorporate into ceremonies or ritual circles or anytime you want to share peace, goodwill, and blessings with others. If there are many people engaging in the ritual, one person can bless everyone, and then one person in the group blesses the first person or you can arrange people in a circle and pass the Chalice having each person perform the ritual to the person next to them and then pass it on.

[this page intentionally left blank]

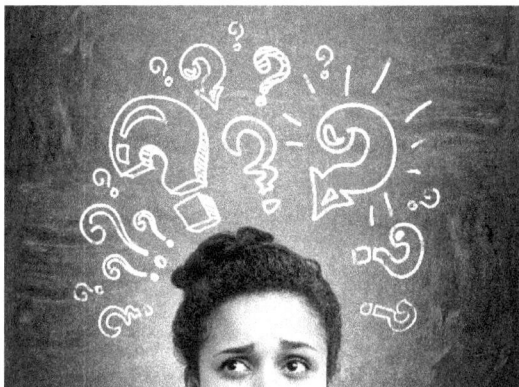

Question Circle for Guidance

"The quality of your life is the quality of your relationships."
~ Anthony Robbins

Time Required: Thirty Minutes

Not sure what else to do to help your relationship, or deciding whether to stay or go in a relationship? Try using a magickal Question Circle. With this recipe you will receive guidance from your own inner wisdom and the guardians of the 4 directions. They will give you information for actions you can take to improve your relationships or to solve a specific problem you are facing with another person.

Be sure to record your results so you will have all the information you receive to go back and look at later when deciding your course of action. You can also return to a Question Circle as many times as necessary for more information and/or clarification on results of actions you take.

Ingredients
- Sun Yellow candle that can easily be carried from place to place
- Wooden or paper matches
- A pen
- Notebook or paper
- Compass (optional)
- A space of 5-10 feet diameter

Recipe Directions
1. Locate the directions North, South, East, and West. Use a compass if you need to ensure you have the directions correct.

2. Create a circle of space about 5-10 feet in diameter.

3. Sit in the South side of your circle facing to the North with your Sun candle in front of you.

4. Light your candle with the wooden or paper matches, hold your hands above and around the flame of the candle and charge the candle by saying:

> *"Child of wonder,*
> *Child of flame,*
> *Nourish my spirit*
> *And protect my aim."*

5. Now take your candle, pen, and paper with you and go sit in the center of your circle facing to the East.

6. Write down your question which for example might be "What blind spots do I have in regards to my relationship with (name)?", "What can I do to improve my relationship with (name)?", or a similar question pertaining to the relationship you are inquiring about.

7. Take the next 3-5 minutes to let the question just sit in your mind. Don't try to answer it, just sit with it.

8. Next, take your Sun candle, paper, and pencil with you and move to the East perimeter of your circle. Set your candle down in front of you and ask the question you wrote down out loud to the East. Be prepared for a flurry of information to come at you usually faster than you can write it all down. Don't stop to think about it, just right whatever comes to you quickly.

9. Start writing everything you get until no more information is coming. Thank the direction of the East and move in a clockwise direction to the next direction which would be the South.

10. Repeat steps 8 and 9 in each direction, moving clockwise to each direction when finished with the previous one. In other words, you will start with East as we have outlined, then proceed to repeat the process with South, then West, then North.

11. After you finish the process with North, go back and sit in the center of the circle facing the East and send thanks out all the way around the circle and blow out your candle.

How to Use the Results of Your Recipe

You receive different types of information from the various directions. This is because the beings in the different directions all specialize in certain areas. For example, the East will give you information about communication, planning and ideas. The South will give you guidance on steps of action to take, willpower energy and desire. From the West you will get feelings and spirit guidance and the North will give you more practical steps to take.

[this page is intentionally left blank]

More Magickal Resources

Kindle or Paperback on Amazon:
1. ***Witchcraft Spell Book Series:***
   - Learn How to Do Witchcraft Rituals and Spells with Your Bare Hands (Witchcraft Spell Books, Book 1)
   - Learn How to Do Witchcraft Rituals and Spells with Household Ingredients (Witchcraft Spell Books, Book 2)
   - Learn How to Do Witchcraft Rituals and Spells with Magical Tools (Witchcraft Spell Books, Book 3)
   - Witchcraft Spell Book: The Complete Guide of Witchcraft Rituals & Spells for Beginners (compilation of Books 1, 2, & 3)
2. ***Kitchen Table Magick Series***

Ebooks and Online Courses at *www.shamanschool.com*
   - Wand: Air Tool
   - Athame: Fire Tool
   - Chalice: Water Tool
   - Plate: Earth Tool
   - Magical Tool: Firebowl
   - Psychic Development
   - Energy Healing For Self and Others

- How to Do Voodoo
- Daily Rituals to Attract What You Want in Life

Find a complete list of magickal resources on https://amzn.to/3swxvPo. These resources are constantly updated so check back often!

Free Gift Offer

To thank you for purchasing this book, I'd like to give you a

100% FREE GIFT

Learn more about your free magickal gift.

Access Your Free Gift at www.shamanschool.com

Find a complete list of magickal resources on https://amzn.to/3swxvPo. These resources are constantly updated so check back often!

About G. Alan Joel

Magick means many things to different people. The form of magick taught by G. Alan Joel for more than 30 years is steeped in tribal traditions from around the world, from both modern tribal cultures and those from the past, which have been mostly passed on through oral dialog.

At the very heart of the magick that Mr. Joel teaches is the use of Universal Laws for the benefit of self, others, and even the planet. These magickal traditions can take on many forms, including simple rituals for daily use, specific spells for particular life situations, the use of simulacra (often better known as voodoo), weather working, water witching, the use of the elemental tools (Firebowl, Wand, Athame, Chalice, and Plate), magickal self-defense rituals, and more. Also included are the use of the Tarot for divination and spellwork, divination rituals of all kinds, Spirit-to-Spirit communication, exercises for psychic development, and abundant healing techniques.

Through his 30 plus years of studying, teaching, and honing his magickal practice, G. Alan Joel has helped thousands of people successfully integrate the magickal, and seemingly miraculous, into their daily lives. In fact, one of the greatest gifts Mr. Joel has offered through his teachings is the ability for his students to always find a magickal solution for life situations that often seem impossible to solve. With magick, anything is possible in the mundane world. All that is required of the practitioner is an open mind, the desire to learn, and a willingness to pay some time and effort into his or her magickal practice. One of Mr. Joel's favorite quotes is:

"What you pay into your practice pays you back!"

While many magickal traditions have fiercely guarded their secrets from the public, Mr. Joel feels that "Magick is the birthright of every planetary citizen." As such he strives to offer magickal teachings that are easily learned and inexpensive (no excessive fees to join exclusive magickal groups or ascend up the levels of learning). He also offers techniques that are usable and effective for all who are sincere in their desire to practice magick. In essence, Mr. Joel's methods teach a form of "Every Man's (and Woman's) Magick." All are welcome, his teachings are simple yet effective, and he also offers online classes in which he helps students troubleshoot their magickal issues in an interactive setting.

Find out more about Mr. Joel's teachings here and on his website (***www.shamanschool.com***) where magickal offerings are updated on a regular basis.

Mr. Joel augments this magickal knowledge and teaching with 30 years of practice as Doctor of Chinese Medicine, including a deep understanding of herbology and acupuncture. His understanding of the healing arts deepens the magickal knowledge he teaches, as magickal healing is a major aspect of his teachings. Mr. Joel believes that while there is clearly a time and place for Western Medicine, magickal and Eastern healing techniques can be harmoniously blended in to offer people many choices for healing all types of health conditions.

About the Esoteric School of Shamanism and Magic

The Esoteric School of Shamanism and Magic was started from a desire for all people from all over the globe to be able to attend a real, if virtual, school dedicated to magick and shamanism. The aim of the Esoteric School of Shamanism and Magic is to help people create permanent, positive change in their lives through the study of esoteric magickal and shamanic knowledge. It doesn't matter what your esoteric background is, whether you started out with witchcraft, religious studies, spirituality or candle magick, we welcome you. We believe that the Truth is the same, no matter which form you practice. We delight in all manner of shamanic schools and traditions, magickal techniques and esoteric ritual. You can visit us at *www.shamanschool.com*, our blog at *http://shamanmagic.blogspot.com*, or on social media via links on our website.

[this page intentionally left blank]

[this page intentionally left blank]

[this page intentionally left blank]

[this page intentionally left blank]